LEADERSHIP
in the trees

Inspiring leadership growth in eight simple steps

David J. Allen

This book is for all the leaders around the world. Remember, never be afraid to learn more, do more or be more!

A special thank you to John Allen, Duncan Scott and Alfred Eden for being willing to share their professional insight and opinions during the writing of this book

Leadership in the trees

David J. Allen

© 2017 David J. Allen.

Summary:

This book serves as a leadership guide to help people maximise their leadership capabilities and capitalise on such in their personal and professional lives. Based on the life experiences and teachings of David J. Allen, a well-known South African leadership coach.

Edited by: Sarah Paterson
Illustrations: Stephen Clark
Typesetting and design: Sarah Paterson
Cover Design: Debbie Solomon Allen

THE AUTHOR

David Allen is an entrepreneur and co-director of Challenge Tours, which runs leadership courses at Greystone Adventure Centre and Camp Solomon. He is the director of the Leadership Training Camp at Village Camp Leadership School in Switzerland and York, England. Every July he leads the Village Camps' award-winning Leadership Training programme based in Switzerland.

As an accomplished motivational speaker and leadership coach, David is in demand both at home and abroad. He has volunteered as a police reservist for more than 20 years and has trained in hostage negotiation and served with specialised units.

David has presented a variety of leadership and development talks to corporates, school groups and police tactical and detective units in South Africa and abroad. He guest lectures at the University of KwaZulu-Natal's leadership and business programme and is a regular speaker at Babson College and Bentley University, two of the leading entrepreneurial and business schools in Boston, USA. He is a dynamic speaker who began his leadership coaching career by presenting motivational talks to audiences of teenagers at Challenge Tours and Village Camps International. In recent years, he has started to address groups from corporate entities which needed to inspire their teams.

Studies have shown that people absorb more information when they are actively involved in the presentation. In light of this, David tailored his interactive approach, which involves active audience participation, to ensure that people retain what he teaches … and he has yet to find someone dozing through one of his presentations!

David is a resident of Estcourt, in the KwaZulu-Natal province of South Africa. He is happily married to Debbie and is the proud father of two. The Allen family is adored by their dogs, Marmite and Charlie, and owned by Cleo the cat *(in ancient Egypt, cats were considered gods… Cleo has not forgotten this)*.

FOREWORD

By Brigadier Duncan G. Scott,
South African Police Services

Many books have been written about leadership. Some authors have taken the time to academically dissect this pursued phenomenon by breaking it down into a science; others would have us believe that leaders are simply born with the natural charisma to lead others. While both of these views hold elements of the truth, the real essence of one-on-one leadership is seen in the pragmatic approach which David has encapsulated in this modest book.

David's approach is simple and keeps to the core principles and values that are founded in everyday life experiences of leaders at all levels. Follow these to become more effective in your journey of leading others!

During my years in the SAPS, I have had the opportunity to work under many commanders but few outstanding leaders. It was the leaders who got the best out of me and have since, even in their absence, played a part in my continued leadership development as I try to replicate their strengths.

What stood out for me most was emotional maturity. An emotionally mature leader encapsulates many of the strengths David teaches in his book. A leader who is secure in themselves does not need to force their opinions on others and draws others to themselves. The great leaders I've aspired to emulate have all had high levels of emotional maturity and have seamlessly applied the very principles which David discusses, to their leadership styles.

The short of it is this: People follow those who truly have their interests at heart, while balancing the needs of the greater group in making the path to achievement that much more rewarding each day. As we continue to mature as leaders, both the positive and negative life experience we gain from working with others can help us improve our leadership skills.

The bottom line is: Treat people with respect. If you think that being a leader makes you superior to others, you're not going to be remembered fondly. Your position reflects your level of accountability and your pay grade accordingly. What you do have a say in is how you will choose to spend your time and treat others. This is what you will be remembered for and what will earn you the respect of those you lead.

INTRODUCTION
Why leadership?

Choose seven national or regional newspapers from anywhere in the world. Read the first six pages and think about what you read. Do you see it? Should we be worried?

The world is experiencing a leadership crisis; not only in politics but in most spheres of daily life. It is as if the elements of good leadership have been lost and there are not many effective leaders to be found.

On a daily basis we see more cases of ineffective leaders being elected to office or promoted to positions of authority because the nominee pool is appalling. The phrases "the devil you know or the devil you don't" and "you have to choose the best of the worst" are becoming all too common.

As a leader, and you will see this as you go through the book, you will learn to create a particular atmosphere, define your desired outcomes and put mechanisms in place to achieve them. Look at history, when the dangerous or risky was undertaken there was always a true leader at the forefront, a person who set an example, inspired the troops and won the day, not just someone who said, "Go there" or "just do what I tell you to."

A crazy example is of British Army officer Lt. Col John 'Mad Jack' Churchill who led his men onto Normandy beaches and through the rest of WWII with just his broad sword. He once captured 42 Germans while armed just with his sword. You see, leaders have a glint in their eye and fire in their hearts. They draw people to them and forge a path for everyone to follow. They exude trust, glow with passion and fortitude. They radiate confidence.

If you successfully embrace the elements of leadership and apply them not just at work, but all aspects of life then you will develop the 'follow me' factor. This is a powerful attribute to have as every day, in all aspects of our lives, we see that leadership happens and that leadership matters.

For more than twenty years I have been blessed with the opportunity of observing a range of leadership styles practised by a variety of different leaders; from corporate heads to national ministers and even a state president. I have also had the good fortune to spend two decades serving with some of the best men and women in the land as a reservist of the South African Police Service. In this guise, I have been privileged to learn from and work with some great leaders and inspirational individuals who I would gladly follow into a firefight. In my civilian guise I have the dual role of leading and teaching leadership.

My business partner, Alfred Eden, and I co-direct Challenges for Champions, which runs leadership camps at Greystone Adventure Centre and Camp Solomon in the KwaZulu-Natal Midlands. I am also a director at the Village Camps Leadership School which is based in Switzerland and England. Through these roles, I've been fortunate to gain invitations to present leadership coaching courses at several universities, businesses and police units and departments around the world.

I don't do these things because I have a divine insight into leadership. I do these things because some great people taught me leadership skills which I successfully adapted to suit various environments and groups of people. What I teach a group of school going teenagers in KwaZulu-Natal will be a bit different to what I teach policemen and women in Boston, USA. However, as you go through this book you will see there are elemental principles of leadership which are universally applied regardless of whether you are a captain of a rugby team or a SWAT team.

Giving instructions is not the same as leading people. We can't all be Winston Churchill or Nelson Mandela, but we can learn some simple philosophies and practical tools to attain the ability to inspire people to do what needs to be done, within a time frame and at the level expected.

By sharing what I have learned over the years, I aim to teach you how to maximise you leadership potential and become a more effective leader in all areas of your life.

I have learned there is one indisputable fact about leadership: Where leaders lead well, people will thrive and where leaders lead poorly, people will suffer. Essentially, success or failure is dependent on the quality of leadership.

STEP 1
The basics of leadership

If I had to ask a group of people what they thought the qualities of a good leader were I'm pretty sure that no matter the group, I would get many similar answers. It is a relatively safe assumption that even as you read this, you will have some of the following character traits in mind, and would use your work environment as a reference. You probably thought of how you would like to be led, what sort of leader you are or what sort of leader your superior is.

You probably thought of qualities such as:

Integrity	Decision maker
Intelligence	Takes responsibility
Self-discipline	Team before self
Strong character	Courage
Tolerance	Good listener
Developer	Patience
Loyalty	Honesty
Respect for others	Proactive attitude

Bearing these traits in mind, as well as any others you may have thought of, can you name a few current or historical leaders who have them? Some of the more popular choices are:

Nelson Mandela	*Ronald Regan*
Vladimir Lenin	*Chief Albert Luthuli*
Chief Mangosuthu Buthelezi	*Adolf Hitler*
Winston Churchill	*Abraham Lincoln*
Mahatma Ghandi	*Vladimir Putin*

Over the years, I have presented many leadership seminars and when I ask my audience to pick two leaders, there are generally two names which are frequently mentioned.

From their moral and humanitarian standpoints, these leaders were polar opposites. We need to remember that for this exercise, we are looking at what made them good leaders, what made people choose to follow them, what their legacy was and even the imprint they left on the world.

After that build up, you may or may not be surprised to note the two leaders in question are Nelson Mandela and Adolf Hitler.

To understand why they were good leaders, we will need to list the characteristics of a good leader and see which of them these two leaders shared, as I have done below.

	NELSON MANDELA	**ADOLF HITLER**
Integrity	Yes	*No*
Intelligence	Yes	Yes
Self-discipline	Yes	Yes
Strong character	Yes	Yes
Tolerant	Yes	*No*
Developer	Yes	Yes
Loyalty	Yes	Yes
Respect for others	Yes	*No*
Decision maker	Yes	Yes
Takes responsibility	Yes	*No*
Team before self	Yes	Yes
Courage	Yes	Yes
Good listener	Yes	*No*
Patience	Yes	*No*
Honest	Yes	*No*

If you add up the scores you will see that Nelson Mandela scored 15/15 while Adolf Hitler scored 8/15.

It is at this point that I ask my audience: "In your opinion, which of these two men is the greater leader?" *Remember, I am not asking who you like or whose moral values you agree with. We are looking at the men objectively to identify what makes an effective leader and not whether they were good and moral men.* We are examining the personal leadership qualities of these individuals and what made people flock to them and follow to their cause. In this study, their causes - whether righteous or despicable - are not relevant.

Look specifically at their leadership qualities. Now, ask yourself **which leader had the greatest following** *and* **how many people were/remain dedicated** *to their cause?*

If you look exclusively at leadership elements, almost every time the answer would be that Hitler was the greater leader; and I'd have to agree with that.

During his time he motivated millions to abandon their principles and commit atrocities in his name.

This now poses a dilemma. We could add many more adjectives and it is likely that Hitler would still score fewer 'Yeses'. So, why on earth would we say he is the greater or more effective leader? Maybe it is time I rephrased the question and asked you to answer this: *What is leadership really all about?*

If we look at the previous exercise, it's clear that one can be a fantastic leader while also being a dishonest, self-serving and arrogant menace to the peace-loving world.

With this in mind, we need to examine some of the elemental qualities of leadership which make a good and effective leader... And no, it has nothing to do with the number of Facebook friends or Twitter followers you have!

Your vision and/or Idea

To be an effective leader you need a clear vision of what you want to achieve. No matter the goal, if your vision of it is crystal clear, you will be able to see how you can achieve it and the basic steps you need to take to do so. You will still have to formulate your winning strategy but you will have an instinctive idea of how you will want achieve it.

Using the Freedom Charter as a moral and political foundation, Nelson Mandela sought to re-write the South African Constitution to include a Bill of Rights for all - and he would settle for nothing less. Freedom, equality and a constitutional democracy were his goals. Hitler wanted the supremacy of the Aryan race and world domination. And if we know a bit about history, he was pretty serious about the methods he employed to achieve it.

I'm sure just about everyone has heard all or part of Winston Churchill's "We shall fight them on the beaches" speech. Here he clearly defined his vision that Britain would never give in to the Nazi war machine. That Britain would never be conquered. In his many powerful statements, Churchill defined what he saw as the only goal possible.

In our day-to-day lives, we don't have to have that much of a radical or long term vision/idea. An objective may be simple, such as convincing your partner to go out to dinner tonight or convincing your friends to watch the movie you want to see.

Anyone with a teenager under their roof will identify with the following scenario. Your fifteen-year-old daughter wafts in after school on a Friday and announces that she is going to the movies that evening. While this isn't quite jack-booting up the steppes of Russia with a Panzer brigade, she pretty much knows what she wants and intends to achieve it. The importance of her initial idea is paramount and the leadership element she used (vision) gives her clear picture of her goal. To achieve her goal, she has a plan to lead the family agenda for that night and had to clarify her vision to make her plan clear to the team (family).

To illustrate this in another way, imagine you were thrust into a game of paintball. The most popular guy in your group may be the best communicator. He's trustworthy, honest and has the patience of a Zen master, but if you ask him: "Hey Bob, how are we going to get that flag?" and he stares at you with the wide-eyed, slightly pale and sweaty look of an infantryman in his first fire fight. I don't think he is the best leader for the game.

His normal self-confidence and eloquence are useless as he is clueless about how he is going to achieve that particular objective. His 'vision' could be clouded with flashes of himself running, ducking, in pain and a lot of confusion. He can't see himself standing proud holding a flag. And this is why he is not the best person to lead the team to achieve that specific goal.

Vision, is the first elemental quality of leadership. To be a good and effective leader you need a goal or idea and you need to be able to see yourself achieving it.

Motivator

Being a motivator is the second elemental quality of leadership. A good leader does more than just motivate people to follow achieve their vision or idea; they also get them excited about it!

To be a strong motivator, you need to believe in yourself and when you do, that confidence shines through. Belief is a vital and very powerful leadership tool. We use it to build strong self-confidence and to share that confidence with others. People know this and instinctively flock to a leader and follow that leader. They will start believing what he believes and they will support their leader while motivating others to do so. If you look through history you will see that every strong leader, regardless of their moral compass, has been followed by a crowd of people who believes what their leader believes. Think of the words fans, followers, disciples, indoctrinated, blind sheep and converts. Whether negative or positive all these words have one thing in common, they describe groups of people who share their leaders' confidence and buy in to what their leaders' goals are.

Imagine your brother is a very negative person. Whenever something is discussed or suggested, he has a hundred reasons why it won't work and why it's a bad idea. Because he does not believe in the success of anything and especially in himself, every decision is clouded by his negativity and his belief that it will fail. Therefore, he gives up easily, is unmotivated and has very little success in his life.

Now picture your sister. She is positive, energetic and literally believes anything is possible. Every decision she makes is made because she knows she will win. She knows she will achieve what she sets out to achieve. She is the family superstar, all she touches turns to gold. Why? Because she believes in herself and her confidence allows her to make good, logical decisions. She does not fear calculated risk and is motivated to find solutions to obstacles.

People want to be around confident people. They enjoy feeling happy. They want to feel like they are part of a bigger picture or that they are achieving something and will readily accept what they plan. People with low confidence and who don't believe in themselves often have a negative outlook. People don't want to associate with negative people and when they do, they are left feeling miserable and eventually start avoiding that person.

Since the last point, Paintball Bob has overcome his sweaty panic and now has a clear vision of how he will lead his troops to victory. All that is left is for him to communicate that vision and motivate (inspire) excitement in his team. Once energised, the team will be ready to win!

There are two ways he can communicate his plan.

1. **If he mumbles, "Umm… well, we could split the team.** Some go left and some go right, someone gets that flag. Erm... I think - well... yes, it might work," he won't inspire much support. I doubt you or anyone else would follow him to a crowded buffet, let alone to what is guaranteed to be a noisy and slightly painful few minutes under fire.

2. **Or, on that hot, dusty day on the range, Bob could** gather everyone around and say: "Right, you three are going to cause a diversion on the left flank. I'll join you with a suicide mission down the centre to draw fire while you two sneak along the right flank on your bellies. Once we engage in a

shouting match about who shot who, the right flank will grab the flag and we'll cover your retreat! It's an awesome plan guys; let's go kick some butt!"

What did Bob do?

In point one, Bob had a clear idea of what he wants but he wasn't creating the excitement or motivation needed to effectively lead his team in the dangerous quest. It seems that he did not believe in himself or that he could lead his teams to victory. In turn, his team was not motivated or that interested in winning. They probably had already decided they would lose.

In the second point, Bob quickly drew you into his imagination, shared his vision and got you excited. You could picture yourself doing what he said you are going to do. This helped you create your own vision and began to generate your emotional buy-in.

An effective leader has the ability to clarify a vision and get you excited about an idea.

After World War I, Germany was left in ruins, its people were destitute. Poverty, hunger and misery were common. Now picture one of those videos of Hitler speaking at gatherings of thousands of Nazis (or quickly look for a clip online and watch it). During these speeches, Hitler would bellow passionately at the crowd. He would share his vision for the Third Reich; a powerful state which was successful, victorious and feared. He used rousing rhetoric and compliments about being the master race and how everyone will crumble before them.

Hitler made his audience feel valued, superior and powerful. He made them feel as if they were part of something incredible and vital - suddenly, they no longer felt like hopeless losers as Hitler was showing them a believable alternative and a better future. This is an example of how the man was a master at the first two elements: Vision and Motivation.

In the lead up to the 1917 October Revolution in Russia, Lenin's power and popularity grew with every powerful speech he made. He uplifted the crowds with his promise of a future of equality and inspired with the downtrodden working class as he ripped into the elitist upper classes. His vision was clear for all who followed him and so too, was the excitement he created.

Think of every leader you know, whether it is a world leader, a celebrity or the average guy on the street who may not even see himself as a leader. They all have one thing in common: The ability to get people excited about their idea.

When people get excited about an idea, they become emotionally involved and invested in its success - they start visualising how they will achieve it and how achieving it will make them feel.

I know everyone has some leadership role they have to play in their professional, social or personal lives. Everyone has an element of influence over someone else. Everyone wants something and will have to lead someone else to attain it. As a parent of a three-year-old, I have a vision of getting my daughter to eat her vegetables. I have to get her excited about my vision. As a salesperson, you have to get me excited about your product. You have to get me to picture myself on that motorbike and tearing up a mountain pass.

It is a common misconception that leadership is only about leading people below you on the ladder: I am the boss, so I lead my staff; you are the teacher, so you lead your pupils. Quite often, one will have to lead colleagues, friends and peers; people who have just as much power or influence as you do.

You may often find yourself having to lead people above you. You may even find yourself leading your leader. My daughter is always trying to lead me (*I have a suspicion that I may not be the real boss of the house; but never tell her I said that!*). My staff are forever trying to lead me towards their goals; extra time off, more pay or getting a pool table put in the recreation room. If your aim is to effectively lead your boss to attain your vision or goal, you will have to get him or her excited about it.

Find your "Yes" people

Leaders surround themselves with "yes" people; these people are your strongest supporters.

When I say "yes" people, I mean those who are enthusiastic about my vision and believe that we can achieve it. If I make what they think is a bad decision, they will automatically discuss it with me and offer suggestions as how to improve. They are "yes" people because they are enthusiastic about the goal and share my determination and belief that it is attainable - it is no longer my goal but our goal.

These people are assets who are on the leaders' side and maintain the excitement. Psychologically, they are vital to influence a group. Humans are social creatures and more inclined to follow, trust or support a group than a lone wolf. Having "yes" people not only maintains excitement but it gives credibility and creates a sense of authority.

Your "yes" people have already bought into your vision and are key to sustaining the momentum. They recruit more support for your idea and even enforce your policies or procedures to help realise your goal. Having valuable backing and encouragement aids the clarity of the vision as well as nourishing the emotional tempo among the followers.

A good example would be a marketing executive who has a clear and viable vision for a project. He has the passion and enthusiasm to create the excitement but needs "yes" people, such as colleagues, to pursue a favourable outcome at a board meeting and gain approval for his venture. Before the meeting, he would engage each of them individually and sell his vision to them to gain their support and he would rely on them to help show favour for the idea.

Think back to Hitler. It can clearly be seen how powerful the winning over and strategic positioning of "yes" men can be to forge a vision. Please don't misunderstand me; I am not encouraging you to form your own private SS to show how good you are at leadership! What I am saying is that if you have key figures supporting your exciting cause, you will be able to lead them, figuratively or in Hitler's case, into war.

Now think of a teenager who wants a night at the movies. She only needs the support of either you or your spouse to get her night out. Getting her mom to agree that as parents, they need a night to themselves might be all it takes to prove her vision is exciting and mutually beneficial.

Perhaps it's your turn to cook dinner on a Friday night. The wise leadership move would be to rope in the kids as excitement and "yes" men to get your partner to treat the family to take-away or a meal out. There is no way I will get my daughter to eat her vegetables if my wife keeps saying, "Oh, she doesn't have to if she doesn't want to." To be an effective leader who attains the goal, I need her on my side; I need her to be my "yes" person.

How it works in real life

Go back to the earlier list of famous leaders and apply the three elements of leadership that we have just discussed. You will be able to see that they apply to each of the leaders.

The leaders had a clear vision of what they wanted. They identified a goal and had a general idea of how to achieve it. They also believed in their vision and as a consequence, were passionate and excited about the idea. And lastly, they were surrounded by "yes" people who drove that idea and grew their support base.

In both the police and civilian world I've worked under management who really didn't have a clue about what they wanted to achieve. Most bad leaders I have encountered were not bad because they made bad decisions and poor ideas. They were bad leaders because they had no idea and made no decisions. If you asked them what their vision was, they would probably recite something from the organisation's code of conduct or say something as generic and meaningless "we have to make turnover this month" or "we must save lives."

They were not excited about their job or an objective. They were satisfying statistical demands and minimum requirements - as long as those were met, they were satisfied. I can assure you they had no "yes" people who believed in their goals, shared their ideas or who offered input when needed. In fact, if you looked at those they surrounded themselves with, you would see they were as negative or as downright destructive as their manager – they were not "yes" people, they were weeds who fed off the negativity and removed the positive sense of accomplishment from the work environment.

To lead effectively you need a vision or idea of your goal. You need to share your vision to get people excited about it and then sur-round yourself with those "yes" people who will in turn, spread that excitement among the group you wish to lead.

STEP 2
Own the outcome

Leaders accept responsibility for, and the consequences of, poor decision making

When I cover this topic with aspirant or successful leaders, we play a version of rock, paper, scissors as a group activity to drive the message home in a very blunt, but simple manner. Everyone pairs up, I go over the rules and then we begin. If there is a draw, a rematch is held until there is a winner and once a round is completed, the losers sit and the remaining winners pair up to compete against each other. The process continues until there is an ultimate champion. Players have to choose from three options: One decision will result in a win, another in a draw and another in a loss. It's that simple.

I've watched these matches countless times and my observations are almost always the same. The winners invariably fist pump with a victorious "Yeah!" before their confident, steely-eyed gazes turn to seek out their next foe. The losers usually mutter something unprintable and glumly accept their fate. It is always interesting to watch a winner, especially as the pressure increases and the competitors thin out. He knows a run of wins can end in one game. You, the observer, can watch how he transforms from an unstoppable and extremely confident force to being eliminated in a single second. The real measure is the conduct of the losers, especially if they have the maturity to accept that they made a poor decision. You may be surprised to learn that the mature losers often show themselves to be the better leaders.

Leaders accept they made a poor decision; they accept they were responsible for the decision and are accountable for the consequences of their decision. They don't blame anyone for their loss. They don't make the excuses people typically make to limit their responsibility and accountability, excuses; such as "it wasn't fair", "I wasn't ready", "I was distracted" or even, "it was the wrong phase of the moon!"

Real leaders don't spend time assigning blame or point their fingers when there is a shortcoming or failure; they accept their role in the failure.

Let's use school children as an example. When they do well, they are quick to jump on podiums and accept certificates. When they do poorly or fail, it becomes the fault of everyone or everything else; the teacher never taught properly, the exam was too difficult or there was an electricity outage (load shedding) that stopped them studying. Name an excuse and it will be used! When I ask students the reason for their successes, they usually say it was due to their hard work. Therefore wouldn't it be correct to state that if you don't do well at school it's probably because you didn't work hard enough?

I appreciate that it is difficult to learn or succeed academically if you have a poor teacher and that it is equally difficult to study in the dark. However, if you put off studying until after you finished playing computer games at 9pm and then the lights go out, whose fault is it your homework is not done? Are you not responsible for your poor prioritisation? Similarly, if you had not paid attention to your teacher's instructions or neglected your school work and failed the year, where does the fault lie? With you or with your teacher? With you! It's your fault for taking 11 months of the year to play games and only deciding to put in the hard work a week before the exams.

Sometime ago, I examined the times in my life when I had got into trouble, when things had not gone my way or I hadn't achieved what I had hoped for. I questioned whether this was due to events beyond my control, decisions that were completely out of my control or whether it was due to a poor decision I had made somewhere along the line.

If a tornado were to come through my leadership camp, leaving me homeless and unemployed, that would be regarded as an act of God - something beyond my control and not my fault.

However, if I was homeless and unemployed due to my poor behaviour in Grade 10, when I thought school wasn't cool enough for me and I failed everything, who is to blame? If I chose to mix with the wrong crowd and chose to be a criminal, who would be to blame for me becoming a 40-something beach bum? The government, my parents, my friends, everyone who never understood me, helped me or gave me what I wanted?

The blame lies with me. I made bad decisions therefore I am to blame.

Let's be honest, we choose our friends and decide on our actions. No one trips over a rock and oops, is in with the wrong crowd and suddenly has a criminal record. The decision was theirs to make.

A simple rule of life: If you are willing to take the credit for the success of a venture, you must be willing to accept the blame and criticism that follows in the wake of its failure.

Here is a real life example. Many high school students attend our leadership camps at Greystone Adventure Centre. As we understand that teenagers will invariably try to smuggle in 'illegals' such as alcohol and cigarettes, we have an amnesty period. At the beginning of each camp, I sit them down to discuss the camp and its rules. I tell them they have until lunchtime to hand over any 'illegals' they brought with them and promise no action will be taken against them. I remind them that once the amnesty period is up and they are caught, they will be removed from the camp, their school will be informed and their parents will have to come and collect them.

Sometimes the children come forward to hand over their 'illegals'. It is heartening to see the maturity of their actions and that they respect the rules of the camp. Nevertheless, we have had incidents where children have been found with 'illegals'. The leader informs me, I inform the teachers and then the parents have to fetch their child. It is interesting to note that these teens are more often than not caught the same way. They don't realise that keeping a secret in such a closed environment is almost impossible. At camp, they share their private space with fourteen others in a hut and someone always lets it slip or reports it to their leader.

The culprits' responses are pretty much the same every time. They are angry with their buddy for spilling the secret. They are angry with the leader for telling me and usually incredibly angry with me for calling their parents as they will be punished. They are usually angry with the teachers because this may affect their school record and they became angry with their parents when they get punished. Honestly, they are most likely to be furious with the whole world when the only person they should be angry with is themselves. They behaved poorly and made a bad decision when they ignored the gift of an amnesty period.

Instead of blaming others for a situation, a good leader will look to himself and evaluate what he could have done differently when things haven't gone according to plan. Once an individual is honest with himself and accepts where and how a problem arose, it will be easier for him to recognise and rectify problematic situations. Pointing fingers doesn't fix anything. Nobody is going to take pity on you. A true leader acknowledges his challenges, acknowledges his role in the challenge and rectifies it.

The application of this principle will ensure your success in life. As a student, if you fail an exam you will not blame anyone but will study harder to excel. As a valued employee, if you fail at a given task, you will accept the responsibility and do what is necessary to rectify it and attain the desired result. As an employer, you will consider environmental factors as well as customer feedback instead of blaming the economy and other influences. This way you will anticipate changes, plan better and grow your business well into the future.

In my business, I have great respect for employees who own up and offer to rectify a situation after when a mistake or a bad decision was made. I find them more valuable if they take ownership of the situation as this means they are unlikely to make the mistake again. Those who try to defer blame and make excuses lose my trust and I have noticed they are often the ones who won't learn how to do things better or differently.

People who have been in business a long time will know that the world does not take pity on you or your mistakes. Nobody rushes in to bail you out of your problem. You have to sort it out yourself. If that means you must call in specialist help or learn more about the challenge, then you do it. A leader takes charge and keeps moving forward. A leader doesn't seek condolences or hugs. A leader does not log into Facebook and post vague and passive aggressive updates to seek attention and affirmation. A leader stands up, takes ownership of the shortcoming, seeks a remedy and strives to succeed.

You can knock good leaders down, but you can't knock them out!

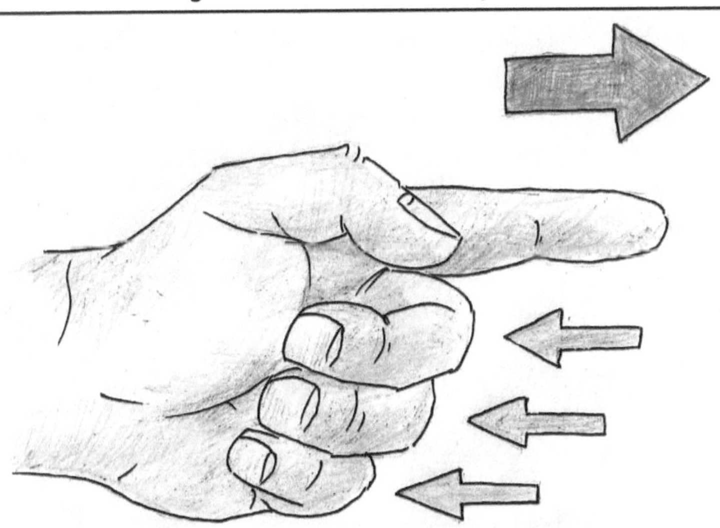

In every situation, whether in my business or personal life, before I blame anyone for my short comings, I ask myself: "What could I have done differently?" There's an important lesson that I learnt in primary school: If you point a finger at someone, there'll always be three pointing back at you!

STEP 3
Your shoes or mine?

"Whenever you are about to find fault with someone, ask yourself the following question: What fault of mine most nearly resembles the one I am about to criticise?"

- Marcus Aurelius, Meditations

Effective leaders walk in other people's shoes

Is leadership easy? Whenever I ask an audience this question almost everyone says that it is and almost all of them feel that they could do a better job than the leaders in their lives.

Generally, an audience is full of nay-sayers and experts on how things should be done. People generally believe that they could do a better job than the president of their country, their boss, a sports star, a teacher or a policeman, even if they have no experience in the specific field.

I'm often most amused by this belief when watching sport. Have you ever noticed how the best players are apparently not on the field but among the spectators? There is always one on the side lines shouting about how he could have caught the ball, would've made the tackle or have scored more points. If this spectator was as good as he claimed to be, why is he not on the field? Most spectators also feel that they would do a much better job of refereeing the game, even though the majority of these so-called experts have never even really played the game at any decent level.

In my twenty one years on the streets in police uniform, I have completed many courses and been involved in a multitude of scenarios from dealing with drunk drivers to handling hostage situations. In spite of my vast experience, I still often encounter individuals who tell me how they pay my salary (a big joke as police reservists don't get paid) and then move on to quote some hash they have heard on a fictional and dramatised police/investigative procedural show. These people honestly believe that what they have learned from the fictional and often highly-embellished TV show. They believe that despite not having my years of experience and training, they are equipped to do my job better.

Employees commonly like to complain about their bosses. I'm sure as you are reading this, you can recall a moment when you complained about your immediate supervisor. You may have thought that if you were in his or her shoes you would do things differently and probably do a better job. Students often feel the same about their professors and teenagers usually think that they are better at parenting. We have all had moments in our lives when we have believed we know better than the referee who is there on the field of play.

As a leader, before I criticise anyone in any position I have to ask myself whether I could honestly do the job and do it better.

I recently had a chap tell me about how he felt under-appreciated at work; about how he didn't like the manner in which he was spoken to, how his working conditions were poor and how he deserved to be paid more. The conversation continued on for a while until he told me about his domestic worker. How she was always wanting days off, more money, how she had made mistakes and then he proceeded to bark at her, in front of me, about something she had forgotten to do. He didn't even realise that the things he complained about in his job and about his boss, he had been doing exactly the same to the person who worked for him. He thought he could run a business better than his boss and achieve staff bliss. In reality he wasn't able to even accomplish this in his own home.

When people are critical of us, we often wish they could walk in our shoes but rarely choose to put ourselves in other people's shoes. Despite our criticism, leaders have to walk in the shoes of others on a daily basis. Effective leaders need to have several perspectives on various problems. As we discussed in Chapter 2, a good leader has to take responsibility to rectify a problem and to do so, needs to evaluate the problem from various perspectives - walk in another's shoes to see the full picture. This process isn't always apparent to someone working under the leader, as they usually only see the resulting decision or instruction.

Brigadier Duncan Scott, former operations commander of the elite SAPS Special Task Force, taught me the valuable leadership lesson of how to put myself in another's shoes. This is an especially good protocol if things are not going as expected, as a leader needs to know what went wrong or perhaps why the staff /employees are not doing what they have been tasked to do.

Before a leader begins to shout at their staff or start thinking that they are all useless;

They should ask the following three questions:

1. Did you understand what I asked you to do?

Unless the leader has effectively communicated his idea (Chapter 1) in a manner that is completely understood and comprehended, there is no way he can expect the desired outcome. The easiest way to test if a subordinate understood the instruction or question is to ask them to repeat it back. Let's go back to my friend's domestic worker. Shouting louder is not going to get your house any cleaner unless the worker completely understands what is wanted and how you expect it to get done. Language barriers may also contribute to the problem. If I ask a cleaner to clean my office, they may understand 'cleaning' to mean: wipe down the desk, empty the rubbish bin and vacuum the floor. I however, may expect it to include the above as well as washing the windows, dusting the curtains and arranging the chairs. The cleaner may believe they have done a great job, while I look over my office and label the cleaner as ineffective. Discussing the expectations or parameters of the task is essential in fostering healthy working relationships with leaders and their staff.

2. Do you have the skills to do what I asked you to do?

You can blast the domestic worker or cleaner for not doing a good enough job but if they have never been shown how to use your state of the art vacuum cleaner or set your fridge to defrost, you cannot expect the outcome you demand. If a policeman is not trained to identify a certain drug, you can't expect them to do it. A good leader keeps his people informed, trained and identifies gaps in knowledge, skills or experience. A good leader uses coaching, mentoring and workshops to develop their people to as high a standard as possible. An excellent leader encourages self-discipline so that his people maintain these high standards. For example: The police's special task force needs to ensure that all its members have the training and skills to do what they are required to do. An untrained unit member would most likely result in a disastrous operation which endangers both their own unit and civilian lives.

3. Do you have the resources to do what I have asked you to do?

If the vacuum cleaner is broken and the cleaner has been requesting a new one to no avail, is it really fair of the leader to criticise the employee's effectiveness? Especially as they were not given the resources to do what they have been asked to do. Policemen, like many other public servants or employees, often complain about a lack of resources. If the job demands a specific tool or machine, you are not going to get it done correctly without it. A leader has to ensure that the employee or team member has the right equipment, in working order and sufficient quantities, to get the work done. Toyota uses the "quality circles" operating procedure. At various times during the day supervisors call everyone together and check if there are any needs. Enough bolts? Broken spanner? Run out of welding rods? Ok, let's sort that out now. (Mind you this also adds to the principle of taking responsibility for success and failure!)

Ultimately, a leader has to know the requirements and needs of all under him or her. A leader must have a knowledge of the work required and must be able to identify challenges or gaps quickly and make decisions. It can be difficult to be a leader. Much is demanded of a good leader in terms of loyalty, dedication and decision making ability, not to mention impeccable integrity and intelligence. Although, good leadership is also about getting the basics right, it's also about having a broad general knowledge and being able to address a challenge from several angles and levels of focus while having the ability to 'figuratively' walk in the shoes of many different people.

I used to be very critical of the medical personnel I saw at accident scenes. As a policeman I would often be the first to arrive at an accident and while trying to assist the injured passengers, I would be infuriated by how nonchalantly the paramedics would stroll over carrying their kit, seemingly without any urgency at all.

In my agitation, I used to angrily tell them to 'move their butts' and even went so far as accusing a few of incompetence. After all, couldn't they see that this was an emergency and therefore they needed to behave as such?

However, in 2002 I completed a basic ambulance course. During this course it was explained that when paramedics get to a scene they should always appear calm and in control. This is essential in helping the patients to feel less stressed; if the medic doesn't appear to be too concerned about the situation, then the patient has no need to be concerned either.

I then realised how wrong I had been in my reactive criticism of the paramedics, without ever trying to understand the reasons for their behaviour.

A policeman friend shared this story with me:

One day, my crew mate and I were on duty when we crossed paths with some suspected armed robbers and a high speed chase ensued. As we were careening after them on a particularly treacherous road (some of the corners were taken on two wheels), the suspected robbers began firing at us. We returned fire while giving chase and the suspects eventually crashed, fled their vehicle and ran through a suburb. We followed; vaulting fences and tearing through yards, while fighting off dogs and irate residents. More shots were exchanged until we eventually cornered the suspects, arrested them and took them to the station. We spent many hours doing the administrative side of the arrest; completing paperwork, impounding their vehicle, booking evidence etc.

Eventually, exhausted, still soaked in sweat and covered in stinging cuts and scratches, we drove to a petrol station. We parked in the shade and removed our bullet proof vests to allow them to dry and bought some desperately-needed cold drinks while we waited for the next call. As we stood drinking and trying to wind down, a middle-aged man walked over and said "I'm glad you've got all day to sit here in the shade; there are criminals out there, you know! Don't you think you should be working?"

I don't think he could have ever have understood, quite how lucky he was, that we had such a high level of self-control in that moment.

STEP 4
Power

If you think being small makes one insignificant, you haven't been kept awake by a mosquito – *African proverb*

Power is not a right - It is earned. The longevity of power is entirely dependent of the actions of the holder.

One of the greatest things a movie director can achieve is to have the right scene, sound, music or moment of silence accompanied by just the right lines spoken in the perfect tone - that is the stuff cinematic legends are made of!

People still sit through several hours of Gone with the Wind, just to hear Rhett Butler growl, "Frankly my dear, I don't give a damn." This scene was iconic in so many ways. It was the first time the word 'damn' had been spoken in film and this gave immeasurable power to those eight words.

Some of my favourite movies (Gladiator and Dirty Harry) have some really good lines in them. It's not the striking phrases themselves which makes scenes legendary but rather the timing of the delivery. You all know the point when the bad guy is on a winning streak, the hero is battling his way through muck and mire when suddenly, with a short speech or statement, he swings the tide of battle or the balance of power.

Russell Crowe's arena speech in Gladiator is a prime example. Picture the scene; he had been demanded to identify himself. He turns around and glares at his arch enemy, Commodus, and states: "My name is Maximus Decimus Meridius. Commander of the Armies of the North, General of the Felix Legions, loyal servant to the true emperor, Marcus Aurelius. Father to a murdered son, husband to a murdered wife and I will have my vengeance… in this life or the next!"

It is at this point in the film when the power swings back to Crowe's character. It is at this moment that the audience feels a tingling in their scalp, grins manically and popcorn chomping skyrockets to 1,000 RPM. It is this emotional build-up that is the pivotal point of the movie as it is when the audience fully identifies with the hero and will almost blindly support his actions and his goals. This is the moment when the stand against injustice takes place. We all despise injustice. As ordinary citizens, we hate it when the 'bad guy' wins and we will generally rally behind the 'good guy' who is prepared to take on said injustice and end it.

One of the biggest problems in society is when an influential leader misuses their power and in essence becomes a scarier version of a school-yard bully. In fact, the only difference between an unjust leader and a school-yard bully is that a bully doesn't have 'heavy artillery'.

We all possess a certain amount of power or influence. Every single person, even those within a massive corporation, has an element of power over another. A humble person in a parts department could bring an entire factory to a halt because they chose not to order a box of bolts. I like to think that I am the boss and the most powerful person in my house; right up until the moment when at 2am my three-year-old wakes up from a bad dream and my wife growls "your turn!"

We all know the amount of power a teenager can wield (sulking, tantrums and emotional blackmail) to compel parental compliance. A school principal has the power to have pupils suspended or expelled, but a thirteen-year-old girl has the potential power to spread a vicious rumour and have him removed from his position. The lesson again, is that we all have power in one form or another.

As leaders, what do we do with the power we have?

Leaders need to appreciate that the power they have was given to them and can therefore, be taken from them. If we were to think of some of the most powerful people at the turn of the century, such as Tony Blair, Muammar Gadaffi, George W Bush and Sadaam Hussien, and ask the question: Where they are now? What would the answer be?

This shows us that power is temporary. It can be given, appointed or achieved but it can also then be taken away in an instant. A president of a country is the most powerful man in a country but on voting day or during a massive uprising, his life's goals and social standing is at the mercy of the most ordinary citizen.

The principle that must be understood by every leader is this: While you have the power to make decisions and influence people, you have a responsibility or even a duty, to use that power positively. You are there to improve the circumstances of those you are responsible for. Your objective is not to become more powerful - that is merely self-serving.

If you look at people who had little military might or political influence but inspired masses to follow them on their mission to make the world a better place, you may realise that some of them actually had more power than emperors and kings.

Princess Diana could not make laws. She could not raise armies or negotiate terms of surrender with Russia. However, she was able to support a cause, such as HIV/AIDS, and with a simple gesture of embracing a person with the disease in front of the world's press, she destroyed society's discriminatory preconceptions. She didn't do this for herself; she had nothing to gain from it financially or personally. What she did do was to take the influence she had, which was built on the love and respect she felt for the common person, and spread it further. What a fantastic example of humanity!

In a single gesture she highlighted the plight of AIDS victims and rallied everyone, from NGOs to scientists, to unite to save human lives. If she had lounged in her palace and ranted and raved on Twitter (had it existed back then) she would have had a similar following to that of a Beverly Hills brat and as much influence.

Princess Diana used the power she had to serve others. In doing so, her power and influence rapidly increased to levels that many world leaders can only fantasize about.

The ideal leadership scenario is when a person in a leadership position, exercises their power or energy in the most appropriate manner to maximise and utilise the potential of their work force. It must also be said that there really is no such thing as president for life. Everything and everyone has a 'sell by' date. Zimbabwe's President Robert Mugabe, for example, made massive improvements in education and commercial industry in his country and in the early 1980s, the country had one of the highest literacy rates in the world. Unfortunately that is no longer the case, as he never conceded to the fact that it was time to step down, and his decision has been to his own country's detriment.

The question good leaders should ask themselves is: "How can I use my power to serve others?" Perhaps the answer lies in empowering their workforce, producing an excellent product or satisfied customers. The interesting thing is, no matter what avenue they decide to take, their service cannot be construed as insincere or as a half-hearted attempt. If you were the CEO of a multinational company and one day offered to make a cup of tea for a cleaner, it would not be seen as a patronising gesture– it would probably take the cleaner by surprise, but it would earn their respect.

Can you imagine the influence and support you would gain, by humbling yourself in this way? Your actions would speak louder than words. Yes, you may have all the power and be able to order anyone to do anything for you, but you chose to make tea for a person who vacuums your office every week. You stepped down from your position of power and privilege and treated the cleaner as an important facet of your world; someone who was worthy of a simple and kind gesture. This is a perfect example of the power of service in leadership.

Most people have heard the biblical story of Jesus washing his disciples' feet. Jesus was the most powerful person in the room and yet he chose to use his power to serve his followers. It is the mentality of 'I'm not too good to humble myself.' This is not a sign of weakness but a sign of strength.

Nelson Mandela, who was the first president of a democratic South Africa, stood down after one term in office because it was what he promised to do and he made way for the next president, Thabo Mbeki, to take the reins of the country. I truly believe that his relinquishing of that power is what made him such a great and highly respected leader.

When the ANC (the African National Congress) became the ruling party of South Africa, there was a push by politicians to have the symbol of the national rugby team (known as the Springboks) changed. Some people felt that the springbok (a small deer, the national animal of South Africa) was a symbol of Apartheid and should be replaced. The South African National Sports Council (NSC) wanted to make the 'King Protea' a universal emblem for all the national sports disciplines.

President Mandela could have followed the popular sentiment and replaced the controversial emblem. Instead chose to use his power, not for his own gain, but for that of the "opposing party" and said: "There is a real possibility that if we review our decision and accept the springbok for rugby as our symbol, we will unite our country as never before" and urged the NSC to approve the Springbok as a symbol of National Unity in rugby which, in 1996, it did

This unselfish use of power by President Mandela, turned many a white South African's negative and distrustful view of him into a positive and accepting one. In my opinion, this was why he was so greatly loved by both black and white South Africans.

A good leader should never let power go to his head. Power is earned and can just as easily be lost.

When a good leader fully understands and appreciates this, he or she will not be arrogant. They will not take their position for granted. They will be more humble and appreciative of their people, staff or customers.

We have seen many big companies expand due to the understanding that their customers were essential to their business and so they treated them well. However we have also seen those same companies fail because they started to take their customers for granted and their service declined.

I recall having endless problems with the telephone company when I first started my business. It was the only telecommunications company in the country at the time and its customer service was terrible. This was probably because their staff knew their customers had no other option and could be treated anyway they wished. Unsurprisingly, when a competitor hit the market the company quickly lost its market share and struggled to stay afloat. The absolute power it had once enjoyed had been taken away from them.

When cell phone (mobile) companies first started operating in South Africa, I remember that the personal service and deals were very favourable for their customers. However, now that these same companies are enormous, it seems that their customers are now just numbers and every deal is structured in the companies' favour. It seems useless to complain, as they are no longer threatened by you taking your business somewhere else; they are too big to care and there will always be a customer to replace you. Most South Africans I speak to have nothing good to say about cellular service providers. Many companies have enormous power but don't seem to realise that unless they start to treat their customers better, the risk of losing their power and market share increases dramatically.

When I was a kid, I enjoyed the monthly trip my dad and I made to the bank to deposit my coins into my savings account. Although I was young, I was always thanked by the manager and made to feel appreciated as if I was doing the bank an enormous favour. I even earned interest and didn't have to pay service charges. These days, that same bank doesn't even have a bank manager at the branch. You have to call a service centre to process any special requests. They charge you a counting fee and service charges every time you need to deposit cash. As a result many people have a huge dislike for the banking system and view them as a necessary evil. These banks have allowed the power to go to their heads and they no longer use it for the good of others.

As I have mentioned, we all have a measure of power and influence over people in our lives and the best way to grow that power is simply to give it away or to use it to benefit others. Sometimes our power is formalised in our positions or titles and other times our power is informal being in our strength to be able to influence others to decide.

For example, most school yard bullies only have power for a few years when they are on top or the big fish in a little pond. When they leave school, they soon lose their power and social standing as they treat people badly. A popular school phrase I will never forget is: "Be kind to nerds. Don't bully them, for one day you will be asking them for a job… Remember, one day the nerds will rule the world!"

When I was a member of the Community Policing Forum (CPF), a man from a local mosque came to ask me for help. Criminals were taking advantage of the Friday afternoon prayers and breaking in to the cars parked outside the mosque. He wanted to know if there was a CPF solution to the problem. As I believe that people of different religions should respect each other's faith and work together, I spoke to the pastor of my church. We decided to ask the Christian community to help our Muslim friends and together we called upon the town's Christians to assemble in the mosque parking lot the next Friday afternoon. For the month of December, we patrolled the lot each week during the Friday prayers and kept the Muslim community's cars safe.

We used our power as community leaders not for our personal gain, but to help others. The response was amazing. The Facebook posts were shared all over the world and I was interviewed by an Islamic radio station which wanted to share the story.

This random act of service had inspired many in both the Muslim and the Christian community. I may not have gained a material or financial advantage from using my power but I definitely increased my power as a member of the community. The recognition generates respect and credibility. This has increased my sphere of influence in the community and my presence as a leader. However, I have to admit, the recognition was bitter-sweet as it indicated how rare acts of selfless kindness are. In this case, I acted out of empathy and thanks to that, the support my business receives from the Muslim community has increased.

If you use your power to just secure your power or to just get more power, you will always be wondering when you will lose your power. However if you realise that power is temporary and instead of using it to better yourself, you choose to use it to the benefit of others, you will find your power increases.

A valuable lesson I learned from practising and competing in martial arts (including karate and MMA) is that you are never on top forever. Train hard, work harder and you have a very good chance of succeeding. However, just because you have won once doesn't mean you will always win. You will win some and you will lose some, but martial arts teach you to never give up.

When you lose you have a choice: Stay down and quit or get up and work harder. You are never a champion forever. One day you can be the best of the best but if you stop working hard and start taking your training for granted, you will quickly be replaced by another champion. Similarly, if you take your power for granted one day you will wake up and it will be gone

---

Everyone has an element of power and the potential to increase it. Power is earned and easily lost. Being rich, bossy or a bully does not make you powerful. One of the easiest ways to increase your power or shift the balance of power is through service to others. Often a simple and selfless gesture can result in rapid gains in respect, power and influence.

STEP 5
Growing your leadership tree

I saw my garden as a symbol of my life. Like a gardener, a leader must take responsibility for what he grows - he plants the seeds and watches them grow and then harvests the results
- Former President Nelson Mandela, Long Walk to Freedom

This is your leadership tree. In this picture, what do you think represents the leader?

A leader does not have a job description; a leader is responsible for nurturing growth.

This is a lesson my father taught me. Picture a simple tree: Roots, trunk, branches, twigs, leaves even flower buds. Now, if this image was a business, where would you place a leader? Take a few minutes to think about it…

The flowers could be the advertising department, with the bees and birds the customers, the fruit could be the product or service. When I ask leadership training teams to do this exercise, I often hear the same answers. Some say that the roots represent the leader as they are the foundation and start of the tree, without them the tree would wither and die. Others say the leader is the trunk, because it holds the tree together and gives it strength and direction.

Others will say the leader is the internal circulatory system which feeds the tree and yet others will say the leader is represented by the top branches because they look down on everything else and receive reports and information.

In my experience, the leader is not part of the tree itself but everything that helps the tree grow. The leader is the sun, water, soil and nutrients. It is the photosynthesis that turns sunlight into food, it is the rain that the roots soak up. We cannot limit the leadership to fulfilling just one function. The leader has to ensure the systems are working with the right inputs and support and has to play different roles.

I'll expand on this example. During leadership camps, I set teams to do raft building. If the leader finds himself occupied with tying knots, he may be a brilliant knot tier, but he is not leading per se. He is not checking if the poles are aligned correctly, whether the drums have been put into place correctly or if the team have their life jackets on. He is tying a knot. He may be doing a brilliant job of tying a knot but he is doing a bad job of leading his group.

Time spent leading versus time spent doing

In my policing experience, a similar illustration of this point is found in a charge office shift. The relief commander must supervise and lead his shift. He cannot spend his or her time loading or correcting entries in the computer system or driving the patrol van. Sure, there may be times when the shift is short staffed and he may have to help in these roles; but he cannot be an effective leader if he is spending his time doing one specific duty.

He has to ensure that his tree grows. He has to get leave forms processed, night shift allowances authorised and manage his team's skill set. He has to be the 'water' of encouragement for the demoralised policeman. He has to be the 'sunlight' of insight at a crime scene and the 'branches' of communication to ensure that other departments like the detectives or crime prevention get the necessary information.

Another illustration could be found in a school scenario where you may have an excellent maths teacher. She could be at the top of her game and be promoted to head of department (HOD). That leadership position has several roles but the teacher could find herself either longing to teach or being unwittingly forced back into the classroom.

Now, if she is spending her full day teaching, setting tests and marking work, as well as handling the numerous relationships, issues or challenges every child has, when does she get the time to lead her department? Is she then just a head of department in name and not in function? How efficient is someone in a role such as this, with so many balls to juggle?

An infantry general's role is not on the front line of a battlefield, even if he is the best soldier there. As a general, his job is to conduct the objective and strategic planning of the army. He should be responsible for managing communications, supply lines and support, such as artillery or air cover.

If stationed on the very front line he may be inspirational to the troops and a magnificent example of a soldier and tactician. If he is positioned where he is forced to be physically involved in combat, he is unable to plan for an enemy attack, he is unable to see the bigger picture and stategise to maintain or regain the balance of power. The general cannot be occupied doing small tasks when he needs to be leading his army.

In a business context, your leader may be the best sales person ever, but if his time and concentration is spent doing sales, the other management functions such as supplies, support, production and human resources will fall by the wayside. I believe the leader must know the role of every employee, to fully understand the function and to have an overview of the business, but he cannot limit himself to being a salesman if he is to lead effectively.

If the need arose one day however, where sales were low, he could step in and pull up the numbers, however he needs to understand that his actual function is still the leader of the business. Just as with the teacher we mentioned earlier. The teacher is a head of department and shouldn't be occupied with a few menial tasks, such as organising a sports day or a school production when there are more important tasks to be completed, such as signing off on reports or managing the staff and their teaching progress.

You need to be able to do everything or at least understand how the components/parts fit together and complement each other. You also need to learn when to step back, delegate and manage the bigger picture.

A friend of mine related a story of when he worked as a salesman at a large car dealership in the early '90s. The dealer principal had started his motoring career as a mechanic and over time he sold cars, got himself into management and eventually rose to dealer principal before becoming a director of the holding company. Despite his lofty position, he still had a working knowledge of almost every facet of his company. He didn't get greasy hands in the workshop but what he did after a technician had been trained to work on a newly released car model, was have the technician show him what he had learnt.

He could go onto the showroom and demonstrate a car to a client and even showed off by remembering part numbers for older models. I was told, there were times when sales were low and he would call up some of his personal contacts to gain a few extra deals for the month and if the workshops were extremely busy (which was most times) would even assist booking cars in for servicing and parking them.

From what my friend said, the boss never tried to be a mechanic or take over the role of a salesman. What he did was keep his senses sharp and up to date with every facet of the company. He did not do this to boost his ego but rather, to ensure he was the best he could be at his job. Furthermore, he could easily lend advice and experience to just about anyone in the business that he spoke to. Apparently, he was a tough boss to work for because short cuts or bull dusting were not accepted as he knew the requirements of every job and what actions or inactions would generate certain results. In that way, he always got the best out of everyone. This is how he ensured that his tree grew.

Leadership is the nourishment that helps a tree (or organisation) to grow and prosper. A leader cannot be an isolated entity within the organisation. He needs to know its structure and how each position within it functions, while overseeing this, he provides the 'water, light and nutrients' needed for growth.

STEP 6
Eating last

I was brought up in a different era. Respect is the key to our culture.

- Chief Mangosuthu Buthelezi

During the run up to a hotly contested national election, we were sent to Nongoma (in the Zululand region of KwaZulu-Natal) for five days. Let's remain polite and say our living conditions may have even been considered less than comfortable by a street person. On the sixth day, the day before the elections, a huge contingent of Inkatha Freedom Party leaders arrived for a massive meeting that was followed by a feast at the convention centre. We were staying next door but ironically, had neither water nor electricity.

So, there we were; unshaven and mostly unwashed, in less than pristine uniforms under the blazing Easter sunshine and watching executive saloons follow each other into the grounds. The occupants dashed from the haven of the car's air conditioner, through the furnace we occupied and into the cool building. We licked our dry lips, looked at our watches and wondered how we were going to hitch a ride to the town to get ourselves some food.

A police VIP guard came wandering up the driveway to the gate we guarded. He was clearly uncomfortable in his suit in the heat. He asked who the leader of our pack was and an old inspector raised his hand. "The boss wants to see you," said the VIP guard and he mooched back down the driveway with the dishevelled inspector following.

It's quite a thing seeing a big man running. Which is why the sight of the Inspector literally sprinting out of the centre a few seconds later and hoofing it halfway up the driveway while waving at us to come down, was so impressive. A mixture of emotions and thoughts ran through me, from a worried "Is someone going to scream at us for looking like we do" to a resigned "Well, what can they do? Send me to Nongoma?"

Arriving at the entrance, we were met by none other than Chief Mangasuthu Buthelezi himself and an elegant lady, who I later found out was his wife, Ma Irene. He shook our hands and welcomed each of us. Confusion set in as our suspicious cop minds wondered what was going on.

As our contingent of about 20 policemen stood facing a hall of immaculate tables, shining glass and impressively dressed guests, as the chief addressed the room in his eloquent English. I can't remember it verbatim but it went along the lines of: "These men have been guarding us and our people for over a week now. The conditions they have stayed in have been hard. They have come from all over the province; have been away from their homes and families to protect us."

He turned to us and said, "Today you are my guests. You eat first. Please enjoy yourselves."

As the shock of the words struck me, a waiter pushed a plate into my hands and pointed me to the carvery. After filling our plates with meat, potatoes, vegetables and gravy, the servers offered us side plates of anything else we wanted. We were then shown to a large table in the front which had been reserved for us. Without hearing a single grumble from the other waiting guests and dignitaries, we sat down and tucked in. The chief himself and his wife came and made small talk; they were even gracious enough to fill our glasses with cold drink. It was amazing.

About half an hour later when we had finished eating, our lead Inspector stood, gave a vote of thanks in isiZulu and showed all the correct cultural decorum and protocol to our amazing host. There were more handshakes and then we returned outside to guard our gate… and with the several cold drink bottles that were handed to us as we left.

It dawned on me that what I had just experienced was the example set by a leader who is loved by his people. Not because he brings them KFC at election time but because he showed genuine love and kindness to the least important people there. Who were we? Just the sweaty cops at the gate, but not to the chief. He valued us and showed everyone that he valued us. The fact that there was not a single objection from any of the other guests wasn't because of blind obedience or fear of the man. The reason was because they had all embraced his values and trusted his integrity. That is what made him a true leader, as opposed to someone appointed to a position to give instructions.

Interestingly, on the other side of the world, the United States Marines have an unwritten rule: Officers Eat Last.

It is a good philosophy to understand that the front line workers are among the most important in a business or even in the police. If a group of constables don't arrive to work a shift, it is a catastrophe for the station and almost impossible to get the job done that day. However, if the station commander spends the day in meetings, the work of protecting the area can still get done.

It is imperative to look after one's staff because they form the foundation of the organisation and resources and support should be applied accordingly.

As leaders we often think that we are the most important people in the business or organisation. We take the best parking spots, have the biggest office and drive the fanciest cars.

We forget that the only reason we get to play golf on a Wednesday is because our staff are holding the fort back at the office. Without them there would be no business.

There is a chapter in the bible where Paul writes about the 'unity and diversity' in the body and the role that different people play in God's plan.

This is found in 1 Corinthians 12 verse 14: *"Even so the body is not made up of one part but of many. Now if the foot should say, 'because I am not a hand, I don't belong to the body' it would not for that reason stop being a part of the body. And if the ear should say, 'because I'm not an eye, I do not belong to the body', it would not for that reason stop being part of the body. If the whole body were an eye, where would the sense of hearing be? If the whole body were an ear, where would the sense of smell be? But in fact God has placed the parts in the body, every one of them, just as he wanted them to be. If they were all one part, where would the body be? As it is there are many parts, but one body. The eye cannot say to the hand, 'I don't need you'. And the head cannot say to the feet, 'I don't need you.' On the contrary, those parts of the body that seems to be weaker are indispensable and the parts that we think are less honourable we treat with special honour."*

What would your organisation look like if you, as the leader, started placing a certain amount of honour on the reception-ist or cleaning staff. If you, as the leader or boss, don't pitch up for work, your business would still operate. But, if your staff doesn't arrive you would have a serious problem on your hands. Your people are an vital part of your business. Treat them with respect.

STEP 7
Constructive criticism

Flatter me and I may not believe you. Criticise me and I may not like you. Ignore me and I may not forgive you. Encourage me and I will not forget you.

- Norman Vincent Peale, The Power of Positive Thinking

A big part of leadership is interacting or communicating with people. As a leader, you will spend a fair amount of time communicating with people - often criticising or complimenting them.

You often hear people say things such as: "I don't care what others say/think." The fact is that more often than not, those people do care and so they should. Criticism is important and if it is given and received correctly, it does not need to be a negative interaction.

To better understand this we need to look at what criticism is and the two more important forms it takes.

In a nutshell, criticism is a form of judgement. Most people take criticism as a personal insult. However, can also be positive. Think of a movie review online or in a magazine – they are not all bad are they? What about the Critics' Choice Awards, to you think there would be such a big deal if it was held to recognise the worst and most negative of the cinematic industry?

Criticism is the analysis and judgement of merits. It can be either positive (*constructive*) or negative (*destructive*).

Constructive criticism often contains helpful suggestions about how a person, organisation, product or service can be improved for the better. It is a form of feedback that promotes communication, excellence and growth.

Destructive criticism is often given with the intention to harm, hurt, trivialise, undermine or destroy a person's self-esteem, creation, work, authority or reputation. It attacks the person, object or organisation as a whole and usually offers no suggestions for improvement.

An effective leader is one who gives, listens to and encourages constructive criticism. Effective leaders use constructive criticism as a guideline for improvement.

Sadly, we can't choose which form of criticism to receive and leaders need to know how to receive, deal with, process and utilise destructive and constructive criticism.

There is an activity I conduct to simplistically demonstrate and provoke thought on the effects of positive and negative criticism. I ask people to pair up to compete against each other. The winners use their fingers to make a "W" on their foreheads and find another "winner" to compete with. While the losers make an "L" and find another loser to compete against. The winners inevitably feel proud and confident as they find another winner to compete against, but if you look at the losers as they fall out, you will see they are less confident and maybe even, slightly ashamed.

As the rounds progress, it is funny to watch how the winners strut around showing off their big "W" and it's interesting to see how the losers of the game head straight for another partner to hide their shame and take a bash at becoming a winner.

These reactions echo real life. When we receive a compliment, our posture changes; we lift our heads and smile as positive endorphins are released into our system. We start to feel good about ourselves. We even associate our good feelings with the person who gave the compliment. We begin to see that person as "attractive", not necessarily in a physical way, but we match our good feelings with them. This also works in the romantic arena. A guy will tell a girl he likes all sorts of nice things to stimulate this feeling. Even small children quickly learn that you are more likely to say yes if they first say they love you and then ask for a chocolate.

The exact opposite happens when you criticise someone. If someone had to come up and say, "Jeepers, your shirt is awful," your shoulders would slouch, your chin would drop and you would frown. When you are criticised your emotional fight or flight system is triggered. Emotional fight or flight is the instinctive and emotional response you have to a negative situation – one that will result in you choosing to remove yourself (flight) from the situation or face it and try to regain control or use it in your favour (fight).

As in the above example, when your shirt was criticised, you will either mentally switch off or ignore the comment (mentally flee) or you will fight back with a snide retort like: "Who died and made you the fashion police?"

However, constructive criticism is an essential part of leadership as in order to improve, leaders have to give and receive feedback. If I'm running a restaurant I need feedback about my food. I need to hear the criticism and know if I need to change anything. I also need to be able to criticise my staff and give them feedback.

As a leader you must know a real danger lurks in over criticising. If you cross that boundary, the desired effect of honest, constructive criticism will be lost. What you think is constructive criticism will be received as destructive criticism (where the subject becomes defensive and their emotional fight or flight is triggered).

Imagine you are at school and your teacher instructs you to stop talking in class. If the teacher said: "Stop talking!" you probably would accept the criticism (reprimand) and stop talking. But if the teacher said: "Stop talking. Every time I turn around you are disturbing the class! What is wrong with you?" Chances are, you would either roll your eyes and mentally flee or be tempted to argue and say something like: "Well if your class was a bit more interesting..." I'm sure you know that the latter would result in a downward spiral and the fact that you were talking in class and when you should have been quiet, would be completely lost. For a more effective conclusion, the teacher could've said something like: "David, you are a very bright boy but you are distracting the others. If you concentrate, I'm sure you will do very well in this subject."

The best way to constructively criticise someone is to start with a compliment, followed by the honest criticism and then another compliment. Do this and you will turn criticism into encouragement.

When explaining this concept to students at Babson College in Boston, one said "so it's like a criticism sandwich." I love the phrase and told him I would use it in the future.

A slightly more complex example of this would be road rage. Imagine we have two drivers. The first (David) who was careless and had mistakenly stolen the other driver's (you) parking space.

In the one scenario, you would hoot at David who would accept the criticism, wave in apology and leave the space for you. The emotional fight or flight response was not triggered and your criticism was clearly passed to and understood by

David. He responded by using your criticism to make a better decision.

In the other scenario, you chose to get angry and started to swear, shout and insult him, his car, his driving and his pet goldfish, Fluffy. David would respond by either yelling back (fight) or ignoring you (flight) - and in both cases, chances are he would keep the parking space.

This brings us to receiving constructive and destructive criticism.

When David stole your parking space and you made him aware of the issue by hooting it presented him with a choice – deal with the criticism constructively (pull out, apologise and move on) or destructively (get angry and attack).

If he decided to react destructively, you would be presented with a choice to remove yourself from the situation (flight) or receive his criticism (fight) either constructively or destructively. Should you decide to react destructively, you will more than likely respond to David's criticism by verbally or physically attacking him. However, if you were an effective leader and understood how to react constructively, you could defuse the situation or turn it to your advantage while, possibly, learning something new.

My business partner, Alfred Eden, always says that the moment you add the word "BUT" to a sentence, you effectively nullify everything you said before that - and he is correct. The words you use are as important as the tone. For example: *That is a great idea and you are very talented BUT I think... In this* example you are about to deliver a back-handed compliment and very possibly imply the person is not talented and that their idea a waste.

Rather use positive, reassuring words when addressing a potentially confrontation issue, for example: *That is a great idea and you are really talented. What do you think of adding XYZ to your idea to further enhance it?* Phrasing your words in such a manner will make the other person feel respected as you recognise them as your equal and their contribution to the issue at hand.

Smiling while speaking is a good technique to use in a confrontational or tricky situation. People respond to positive and non-threatening expressions and body language; a simple smile will help those you are speaking to relax and focus their attention on what you are saying. As your smile tells them that they are not under attack, the emotional fight or flight response is not triggered.

There is no doubt - the manner in which you treat someone, when addressing an issue or giving criticism will determine the outcome. My advice is that as a leader, you should use the compliment trick (it helps people save face) and to never forget the power of the smile... but more of that in the next chapter!

Keep it constructive

It's not always easy to accept constructive criticism as it is intended, so I have compiled a list to help you in such situations.

- Stop your initial reaction

- Remember the benefit of feedback and make sure you understand what you are really being told

- Ask questions to deconstruct the feedback to ensure understanding

- Don't make excuses, ask for suggestions

- Thank the person for being honest and bringing it to your attention

- Ask for time to follow up

- See if there is truth to the matter and if there is make a game plan to sort it out

- Remember constructive criticism can benefit you

STEP 8
Respect

A leader must look and act the part

- David McCollough

If you had to ask a group of your friends how they wanted to be treated, you would probably find that about one in ten would say they wanted to generally be treated "well", but the vast majority will flat out say they want to be treated with respect. The problem is that many people will wait for another person to show them respect before they reciprocate and while the other person is waiting for the same thing – neither wants to be the first to show respect. In the end there isn't much respect either way.

One of the most interesting SAPS training courses I have attended was the hostage negotiation course, where the instructor impressed on us that as a negotiator, you have to immediately gain the respect of the hostage taker. If he doesn't respect you, the hostage could be killed within minutes and even more lives could be at risk. To put that in a timeline, he told us that you have literally 30 seconds to make a good first impression and gain someone's respect.

As intuitive as they might think they are, most people will judge a person they first meet almost immediately. (Women, it seems, always notice a person's fingernails and shoes) So, how do you make that first really good impression if you only have 30 odd seconds to sell yourself? It's helpful to note that the words you use only make up 10% of the impact of communication.

As an example, if I stood with my hands in my pockets, staring at the ceiling and greeted you with a monotone "Hi my name is David I'll be your speaker today I hope you enjoy..." line, you would probably not be very impressed.

It is important to note that the tone of your voice makes up 30-40% of the impact of communication. If I greeted you with my hands in my pockets and still no eye contact but spoke with more enthusiasm: "Hi! My name is David, I'll be your speaker today and I hope you're going to enjoy yourselves!" chances are that you would be more interested.

About 50-60% of the impact of communication is actually nonverbal. If I were to say that same sentence again but smiling, gesturing in welcome, making eye contact and looking at my audience this time; I would make a much better first 30 seconds impression .You can see that if I just relied on the words alone, I would never make nearly the same level of impression or impact of communication. It's important to remember that people base their judgements of you not on what you say, but more on how you say it and even, how you look when you say it.

At our leadership camp (Greystone Adventure Centre), the bus transporting students takes roughly thirty seconds to drive from the entrance to the parking area. I can be assured that each child coming in will make that thirty second judgement of the camp, even before they climbed off of their seat. Now the camp itself cannot talk, it's a physical property, but things like the neat gardens, the well maintained buildings and smartly dressed instructors waiting for them will communicate a good first impression. You can well imagine, however, that if a bus arrived to long grass, broken windows, and graffiti painted on dilapidated buildings and ragged looking; unshaven instructors with cigarettes hanging out of their mouths, most of the kids wouldn't even get off the bus.

A big part of making a good first 30 second impression and gaining respect is your use of manners and especially how you greet someone. *Manners maketh the man*. I there is no such thing as "old school" manners there are just good manners. This means that how you great someone often makes the greatest impression.

In South Africa we would not be too fond of a first time greeting being a massive hug and kiss on both cheeks. For us, a sincere handshake would be more appropriate. Now, taking our varied cultures into consideration, how do we do that so as to make the most positive impact?

The best I've come across is what one of my mentors, Mr Phil, calls a "webbie". The shake is firm, right up to the web between the index finger and thumb. You go "webbie to webbie when you shake hands.

Always touch webbie's. No bone crunching (physical strength has nothing to do with intelligence or integrity), no sloppy fish limp grips, and no vigorous up and down water pump cranking either. Your hand should be extended (not thrust like a sword) perpendicular to the ground, with your wrist cocked slightly down. A hand extended flat with knuckles up can appear dominating.

Maintain eye contact and use the person's name, "Good to meet you Mr Khumalo." And SMILE. A genuine smile releases endorphins into your body. When you smile at someone it has a reciprocal effect. A smile is contagious. So when you smile at someone, they will in turn smile at you, causing positive endorphins to enter their Body, causing a positive feel good moment for them. They will associate their positive feeling with you, making you seem more attractive. Not necessarily physically attractive, But they are likely to like you just a little more.

Also, using the name of a person the first time you meet them helps you to remember that name, and, use the name you are given for the other person. If they are introduced as "Dr" Singh or "Reverend" Visser, use that title and name unless invited by the person to use another.

A good greeting is an automatic acknowledgement of respect, indicating 'this is who I am, let's get along'. Military worldwide uses a salute to not only greet officers, but show deference to that person's rank or status. The salute, albeit in slightly different styles, is raising your right hand (left arm straight by your side) until your fingertips touch the brim of your cap or beret. (Some forces salute without a headdress on.)

You hold that pose until the other person has acknowledged the salute by returning it. It is interesting that across the world, with so many diverse cultures and nations, the salute is a uniform standard of greeting in police and military circles. More interesting to some is where it originated. The version I understand is where medieval knights, who were covered from top to toe in armour, would raise the visor of their helmets so that they could look each other in the eye, as well as showing their face, showing that they are who they claim to be and haven't got someone standing in for them. The visor was raised by the right hand, further showing at that time that their fighting hand was not holding a weapon. This symbolism extends to the handshake. We shake right hands as a symbol of "I'm holding your weapon hand and you mine." It is worth noting that Boy Scouts shake left hands as their motto is "be prepared". It is in the motion of raising the visor to make eye contact, where we get saluting from today.

When you meet someone, especially for the first time, you should stand up and remove your hat (in the civilian world) and sunglasses so that you are on the same eye level of the other person and you make that critical eye contact. If the other person is in a wheel chair, you still stand up but bend to shake their hand if offered.

Some people have massive stigmas attached to quad/paraplegics, believing they are sick or in some way contagious. This is massively degrading and disrespectful. Even a quadriplegic will attempt to offer you their hand. Take it gently and respectfully. Look the person in the eye and, as above, repeat their name. If a person is on crutches, wait for them to gain their balance and free up a hand. If they are unable to, keep your hands by your side and greet.

What if the person is an amputee? Again, they may offer you their left hand. This may seem awkward to you. Do not give them an upside down right shake, but use your left hand and LOOK COMFORTABLE DOING IT. You may one day have to go for an important interview with a differently abled person and I can promise you, your actions will be watched very closely and analysed.

In modern times, in order to gain that vital 30 seconds, you have to put aside all fears or prejudices.

There is never a better time to learn a little about different cultures than yours. For example: If you are meeting a Jewish Rabbi for the first time, be less afraid of doing something wrong, rather be conscious of getting the basics right.

A police friend of mine was called to an armed robbery at an Islamic bank. Although nobody was seriously injured, there were several staff members who were highly traumatised. One was a heavily pregnant lady.

What earned my friend a commendation letter from the head of Organised Crime and the director of the bank?

He summoned an ambulance and ensured that the controller made sure that the paramedic was a Muslim. He knew that a Muslim woman may only be examined by a Muslim paramedic or doctor.

You see, it wasn't about "sucking up" to another culture. It was about being as professional as possible, rendering the best possible service and showing respect for another's beliefs and culture.

The same friend helped recover a stray dog out of a cemetery. A neighbour's dog had escaped his yard and found its way into the property of a local mosque and then cemetery. He knew that it was very distasteful for an animal to be there so he made every effort to lasso the dog, get it off the property and greet the Imam. Result? A huge deal of mutual respect and understanding between the SAPS and local Muslim community developed.

In talks, I ask women what they should do if a man opens a car door for them. Not many know the answer is to reach across and unlock or open the door for him. Usually, they are coo-ing and aah-ing while settling into the seat. The adjectives that do come to their mind about the man though are integrity, selflessness, honesty and respect. Why? Because people associate those adjectives with a polite and well-mannered young man.

Strictly for educational purposes (*I swear!*) I would find myself watching the Jerry Springer show. For a moment let's put aside that the people may well just be actors, but if you could picture the average guest on the show. The dress code, levels of hygiene, let alone depths of depravity and promiscuity are something to behold. More often than not they end up shouting and swearing at each other and badly coordinated punches are flailed. But one line kept coming up show after show, "You don't show me no respect!" (Forgive the double negative) I sit there thinking, lady, how could you demand respect, or even show it, if you clearly haven't a shred of respect for yourself?

There is a big difference between fear and respect. A bully in whatever guise may demand "respect". But that is gangster-speak. What they want is for you to fear them. Avoid such people. They will never add any real value to your life nor will the respect ever be mutual.

Interviews, especially job interviews are places where your 30 seconds impression could not be more vital. Your dress code is a means of communication. You have to dress according to what is appropriate for the interview or position.

You may be the best engineer for a job but if you arrive in beach shorts, a sweaty vest and flip flops that job will go to someone else, however less qualified. The interviewer will believe that if you cannot look after yourself, or cannot be bothered to look presentable, you will not look after the project nor produce it at the quality desired.

If you act like trash, and dress like trash, don't be surprised when people treat you like trash. If you are swaggering around with your underpants showing and your cap on sideways, using swear words like a comma in a sentence. Don't be surprised or complain when no one takes you seriously.

I often tell young people that if you wanted to be treated like a queen or a king, you must conduct yourself like royalty - with humility, respect and kindness. If you want to be seen as the life of the party, the fun person or the adventurer, you have to conduct yourself as such and not as a wallflower which is present but unnoticed.

If you want to be taken as a serious business person, you need to present yourself as one; be confident and don't run yourself down. You need to be the sort of person people would want to invest in or support - you must inspire trust and confidence.

Seriously now, put all the PC and participation-trophy thinking aside. Now ask yourself: If I had to invest my salary for the entire year before I received it, who would I invest it with? The first guy you see arrives in a filthy dented and old car. He is wearing creased clothes with an expensive but battered watch and swaggers into the room swearing, burping and laughing about how much he spent getting drunk or shopping and how much he lost on the horses.

The second person arrives. She is a confident young woman who walked in with tidy hair, a laptop and a briefcase. She has clean fingernails, her clothes are ironed and she speaks in an even tone, greats you and starts presenting clearly-explained options, risks and rewards. Her car is not flashy but clean and well cared for. So, which one would you pick? I know who I would do business with. As much as we hate to admit it, how we show ourselves to the world influences how we are seen. People don't have x-ray vision and can't "see the inner you!"

Sometimes I am asked "Sir, when do you stop showing someone respect?" I will then ask the speaker what their thoughts on the question are and the answer mostly received is: "When they no longer show you respect." And I think that's true for most people. One of the biggest lessons on respect, and humility, I learnt while on duty in the SAPS, was by Nelson Mandela. I was part of a Police security team when he flew in to a venue for a high level meeting. He got off the helicopter surrounded by guards and VIPs and as usual greeted everyone in the area. He reached me, looked at my uniform then greeted me,

"Good morning Mr Allen, how are you sir?" I was stunned; the president of our country was calling me sir! Next he asked, "Mr Allen, can I lean on your arm?" Of course, I obliged and there among all the brass and rank, Mandela walked to the building resting on my arm.

The day dragged on, we did our perimeter checks, made our reports and the temperature soared. At one stage a box came outside and in it were a stack of cold drink cans. We each took one and grateful for the liquid sugar, carried on the routine. Eventually everyone was leaving and we formed up correctly to see Mandela off. He came out and shook hands with everyone again, making his way to the chopper, engines already running. He got to me and with a handshake asked, "Mr Allen, did your men get their cold drinks?" I nodded yes and bade him farewell. (I had a bit of a chuckle as 'my men' were mostly higher rank than me).

Then it hit me as the bird rose, carrying him away. Of all the things the president of South Africa had to think about and talk about that day, such as education problems, economic solutions, racism issues, among all the answers he gave and questions he posed, he was still sincerely concerned about whether or not I, a relative nobody, had received a cold drink. He actually took the time to make sure the policeman got cold drinks.

Pondering this more made my head spin. Here was a man who, if I looked in the mirror, had been locked up and persecuted for the better part of his life by people like me; the stereotypical young, white male policeman. Yet here he was, one of the most powerful men in the world at the time, showing me respect, and he ensured that I got my can of coke. Something I could not dare demand from such a figure.

It taught me humility; I learned that no matter who you are or what position you hold, there is never an excuse not to be respectful or not conduct yourself with dignity. After being imprisoned for 27 years by men like me, I believe the answer to the question of when do you stop showing others respect, to be: never!

My other favourite Mandela story is when I was part of a convoy moving him in Durban. Our day's detail was assembled at the hotel and then briefed by the senior close protection officer. The usual deal for transporting any VIP of that level is to plan the route in minute detail, maintain motion, have traffic blocks cleared by outriders or prepared static officers and keep the process as seamless as possible. (The modern high speed convoys are, in my opinion not only unnecessary but reckless). This time we were in for a shock. We were ordered, (and this order came from the man himself), that we were to stop at every stop street, We were to stop at every red traffic light, We were to implicitly obey every rule of the road from indicating to maintaining safe following distances.

You see, Mandela's ethos was that if he could not respect even the most basic traffic rules, how could he expect the citizens of the country to obey greater laws. As the president of the country, If he could not respect other road users, how could he expect anyone to respect him? Mandela's philosophy rubbed off on me in a big way. You don't just show respect for people higher than you or greater in stature. You show respect for everyone, as everyone has value and is deserving of being treated in a dignified and respectful manner.

If you consider yourself to be a respectful person, then Show the same amount of respect to the cleaner as you would to the CEO.

YOUR LEADERSHIP CHEAT SHEET

Core lesson: To lead effectively you need a vision or idea of your goal. You need to share your vision to get people excited about it and then surround yourself with those "yes" people who will in turn, spread that excitement among the group you wish to lead.

Core lesson: You make your decisions; make sure they are informed decisions. Be prepared to accept responsibility for them and be held accountable for the consequences. A good leader will do that - learn from the mistake or error in judgment and formulate a new plan to achieve the goal. A poor leader will blame everyone and anyone instead of asking himself, "What could I have done differently?"

Core lesson: Good leaders take the time to fully understand and appreciate a situation. They try to walk in another's shoes before they are critical of another's actions. Never be too quick to judge.

Core lesson: Everyone has an element of power and the potential to increase it. Power is earned and easily lost. Being rich, bossy or a bully does not make you powerful. One of the easiest ways to increase your power or shift the balance of power is through service to others. Often a simple and selfless gesture can result in rapid gains in respect, power and influence.

Core lesson: Leadership is the nourishment which allows an organisation to grow and prosper. A leader cannot be a single entity of the organisation. Instead, a leader needs to intimately know the structure and how each position in the organisation functions, while overseeing it and providing the water, light and nutrients the tree needs to grow.

Core lesson: What would your organisation look like if you as the leader started placing a certain amount of honour on the receptionist or cleaning staff? If you, as the leader or boss, don't pitch up for work, your business would still operate. But if your staff doesn't arrive you would have a serious problem on your hands. Your people are an important part of the body of your business. Treat them with respect.

Core lesson: If you consider yourself to be a respectful person, then Show the same amount of respect to the cleaner as you would to the CEO.

KEEPING IT CONSTRUCTIVE

It's not always easy to accept constructive criticism as it is intended, so I have compiled a list to help you in such situations.

1. Stop your initial reaction

2. Remember the benefit of feedback and make sure you understand what you are really being told

3. Ask questions to deconstruct the feedback to ensure understanding

4. Don't make excuses, ask for suggestions

5. Thank the person for being honest and bringing it to your attention

6. Ask for time to follow up

7. See if there is truth to the matter and if there is make a game plan to sort it out

8. Remember constructive criticism can benefit you